Magic Seeds of
Personal Destiny

by Daniel James Glass

Magic Seeds of
Personal Destiny

by Daniel James Glass

Magic Seeds of Personal Destiny

ISBN: 978-0-578-70016-8

Cover art created by Daniel Glass

contents:

"To realize one's destiny is a person's only obligation."

- Paulo Coelho, from *The Alchemist*

This book is dedicated to my family.

I want to thank; my parents, my brothers, my daughter, my sisters in law, my parents in-law, and most of all, my wife Abby. Thank you all for your support of my work and believing in me.

Foreword:

While I intended to write an altogether different book, I felt pulled throughout the writing process towards what had become this precious book. It is only here because I have followed the lessons discussed throughout these pieces of poetry.

My goal was to create poetry to look at the world more abstractly, even if it remains ambiguous. I hope you will find yourself in these pieces, and you feel their magic as you read them.

- Daniel James Glass

I – the Integration of Broken Blessings

New Year's Day

New Year's Day
and the spread is spoiled,
a unicorn horn sticking out
turned out to be a pigs tail, tenderly uncoiled

electric, this once was
now it feels flaccid, quickly losing charge
like a branded piece of history
or a seasonally slaughtered hog.

In case I have been mistaken,
it's as sobering as the clear-cut date,
that it's time to resign my position
and move on as the new decade awaits.

Money is just a stock prod
moving the herds along,
it pulls at the tails
of the meandering swine songs,

but no squeals are necessary
when it's time to trim the fat
and retreat from the monotony
when the herds head toward greener grass.

Slay the dream of what this once was,
the favored thoroughbred of the sky,
is speeding towards the ground now
because all fat dreams must die.

You have to heal yourself,
because everything else can be taken away from you.

Immobility

It used to be hard for us to sit still
we preferred motion, we preferred being busy,

we were trained to be efficient
with the decisions involving the body,
involving the heart,
involving the mind,

but this new immobility
is forcing us to confront all of the ways
we would compensate
for the things that we felt
that we had lacked,

this new immobility is
forcing us to confront
the wounds we avoided
and the belief that our self worth was determined
by how efficient we were with our time.

We used to prefer motion,
even if we knew
we were just moving in circles
but we no longer do,

that old cycle is broken
and its break is closer to its mend,
a beautiful attachment connects us
to where these old ways now end,

this forced pause,
is causing the world to reset
helping to steady our focus,
on where our energy should be spent.

Giant Black Seed

I have a giant black seed.
So big, I am not sure if it will grow.
But if it does, everything will change.

There are so many ways for it to branch out,
it will need time to expand,
it will need a lot of light
and take a lot of grounding work.

I hope it is not dug up too early,
it has grown out everything that I have learned,
and it will rise in ways that I don't know of yet,

it will take an act of God,
and the secrets of spirits
whispering through the wind,
for this grown seed to light up
in passionate flames,

others will see its smoke
and I may be forced to clear out
of places where I had once felt safe.

I have this giant black seed
it looks like a giant orb
and in it, I can see the future.

For now,
it is still forming in the pits of my gut,
fed from the blood flowing out of my chest,
while my heart flutters and my soul radiates.

the Caverns

You are a canyon of curiosity,
and a mountainside of beliefs
but there are hallowed grounds existing,
inside of your wood covered peaks,

If you can venture
into the layers of yourself
you will find dark passages,
that lead you to beauty,
deep underground passages
that dictate
the way you interact
with the world around you.

Gentle streams pull the pieces
of crumbled secrets,
of forgotten dreams,
of ashamed tombs,
and flowing beliefs,

Those caverns of your self
hold elongated shapes
of what is really there,

Just shine a light
onto the mystical nature
of those old mysteries,
in those shadowy caves,
the places you have chosen to forget,
and you will find complexities in the types of quiet
that won't see the light of the day,
there are places where silence has become so intense
you can hear it ringing now, as a sound.

If you can shine a light on those old faces
on those hardened crystallized feelings
rising from the earth,
then you will also see the potential
reaching up towards you,

By accepting the dark places that exist within yourself
and not keeping them in the dark,
you can heal.

By putting light
to what they are,
and letting old meanings
be redefined,
you can come back into your life
uncharged and unaffected by the ugliness
that will try to greet you
in the most transparent illuminations.

Inside,
you may also find the diamonds
you left behind,
jewels of uncertainty
once categorized and covered up,
you may hear
the delicate drippings of eternity,
echoing from your soul
to the center of the world.

There is beauty in discovery,
both finite and infinite,
you have access to the lessons of the universe,
you are a creator,
you are your own saving grace,
you are magnificent
in every way that exists.

The stage is set.
The sun is the spotlight,
the mountainside casts
shadows both day and night,

But if something is caverned out of sight,
eventually the unsettled and unresolved part
will rear itself up high and afraid,
until you dig in to see the way,
it once trembled.

You are your only enemy
and you are your biggest hero,
but your existence is a mountain of lessons,
it rises to the world by collision
from the memories that are unexamined, underneath.

Sparking Away

I am not the type of person to smoke cigarettes,
although I have before.

They felt good. My mind was free.
I could smoke three or four in a row, until I was dizzy.

No,
I am older now and I worry about my health.

I am the type of person to grind my legs up,
to run until I puke,
to ride a bike until I am dizzy,
to run a marathon so hard
I fall at the finish because my legs no longer can hold me up.

Lungs burning,
arms tingling,
body abused,
my heart races with the same blood still.

I still burn through this life that seems too long.
I pound through the early morning alleys and late-night parks,
sparking away in the corners of dusk and dawn.

I have done this for long enough
that I feel like I have died a few times,
yet, I still head back out the door for more pain each day
no matter the weather, my body will pull me outside to do it.

In the cold winters
and the blazing heat,
I take shallow breaths
and my body slenders in its frame.

It seems like a rebellion,
a revolt against absurdity,
the labored breathing
never really goes away.

Whether I'm burning with purpose
or longing to escape,
I still set fire to the things
that I cannot change.

a Spider web

I am sitting out on the porch
on the corner of my deck,
there is a water drain there in the upper corner
with a thick spider web spun over it,

it silhouettes across the night sky
the stars cause its thin threads
to shimmer,

there is so much complexity up there
but a hard rain could wash it all away,

it is beautiful
this little beast's creation,
nature's tiny engineer
it must take hours to spin a home like that,
some interwoven folds
across the grids of space-time.

The cycles of life spin around us,
across this planet,
wild criss-crossing lines holding everything together.

Life moves here,
it dies here,
and someone ends up wrapping up what is left.

I am not sure where I fit most of the time,
on this big piece of rock
created from the explosion of stars,
put in place by some engineer, a map maker,
charting out my beauty and faults,
spinning from the challenges
of the human heart.

Whether from the stars or the threads
that are interwoven between us all,
life is a miracle, no matter how it chooses to be,
sitting back in a king's high chair,
or scaling the heights of this world
as a dangling, eight-legged, dark serenading dream.

Forbidden

Forbidden fruits,
forbidden truths
are always there,
but can be buried underneath the woods
surrounding you.

Over time,
common fears
started commandeering your growth
scaring your individuality, into retreat.

You should revisit each fear,
that is towering tall,
and cut them down
one by one.

Cut down the woods,
eat the youthful fruit,
and remember to accept everything
that is surrounding you.

Do not forget,
that there is always a balance,
the light reaching branches
creating a shaded seat,
for the infestations of bugs and birds
occupying your retreats.

You are both the good apple,
and the rotten peach,
you are the cut-down forests,
and the overgrown leaves,
you must allow all parts of you to be.

Do not reject your exotic sparks of brilliance,
or the harshest teachings
that came in your unique defeats,
you must be selfish to grow
and sometimes be the monster,
your life requires you to be.

To be whole,
means to stick out for who you are
and who you are not.

You are the spaced out sparkle of the stars,
you are the perfect destruction,
you are more than what you see,
you are everything that you feel,
your thoughts rocketing up first,
then the world sends those wishes right back to you,
re-affirming your beliefs.

You are a seed of creation,
you have the energy of the stars burning inside of you,
it is never a better time,
for you to accept these truths.

Like Atlantis
or a dream forgotten,
choose to rise again,
and grow up as a healthy three hundred-foot
redwood tree,

so that you can stand proud,
like the Statue of Liberty,
waving out to everyone,
the brightness
of opportunity.

Younger Again

If I could talk to my younger self again,
I would not have spent so much of my life
fighting to remember that I am still,
who I thought I was back then.

This crooked crown and all,
wide grinning and shit-kicking,
I am powerful enough to startle you
when I open my mouth to roar.

If I were younger again,
I would accept this person I believe I am,
and accept the knowledge of infinity
I feel inside of me,

An extension of divinity,
we are internal,
eternal royalty,
I am a lion,
not some parlor tricked identity,
I am my own king,
harnessing the winds of destiny,

With the push and pull of virtue
I remain wise,
I only strike to survive,
and do it all with my pride,
my mane, my majesty,
with this royalty I can feel inside,
of the mystic reign.

Nothing makes me feel more alive,
then my gut and these roaring forces
I feel from deep inside.

Yes,
I can belt out a roar
from the magic and majestic things
that existed before this life,
and the memories of my own mind,

I am limited only by time,
but free to dream,
and destined to live freely,
haunting visions of death and doom,
still trying to render my perspective blind,

but I can see the future
it is so bright, full,
and shines so radiantly,
because this world
is a product of the collective,
we are all God
and we are all sublime.

Fire-bellied Bravery

Big fires used to burn,
I would hold them behind my teeth,

until the tongue tied hell starting spreading,
and big winded, fuming bouts would release,

but the more self work I do,
the more the fires seem to cease,

with the trauma now resolving,
my hot iron tongue cools in peace,

I found a fire-bellied bravery,
from my smoldered out beliefs,

nothing ignites me like it used to,
so I can keep the fiery stokes at ease.

Some things are always there
living in the very fiber
of your soul.

Spiraling Melody

Destiny dances
to a spiraling melody,
echoing off in the distance,

it sometimes soars
in winged flight,
spreading in the wind,
from a powerful wish,

it flows around you
as sparkling crests of the future,
rippling across the open plane of water,
like little reminders of the possibilities that can come,

it is from the figure eights of your drive and purpose,
that life can slingshot change,

A transcendent dandelion wish
that ripples across the ocean,
below the fortified masts
and sailing thoughts of aged woods,

this prophetic whisper blows in the wind,
and this air of a greater purpose,
keeps howling to me much stronger,
than I ever thought it could.

Grandmaster

I sat stone-faced
awoken in the night,
this nightmare
was taunting me,
making it hard to breathe.

A hooded man was in the center of this room,
this giant stage where the curtains were drawn,
surrounding him was everyone that I know,
and the man was there in silence, just spinning around,
pointing to each of us as he spun, as if to say,
that one day, he will come back for each of us,
the spotlight following where he was pointing,
the crowds would gasp when the spotlight would shine on them,

I bobbed up for air,
up and out of my sleep,
like the Navy Seals will do in water,
hands tied behind their back, one giant breathe
before going back under the surface,
touching the bottom of the deep end of the pool
and flutter kicking up again,

I realized that the more I can embrace our meeting
as an eventual fate, the better that I am for it.
I am now stronger because of this dream.
That angel of death was there to warn us,
to remind us that he is always near.

I fall back asleep, continuing to dream
and by the morning I had embraced this certainty,
that death is always there
forcing me to be my best,
a director on this stage

a conductor of the big string movements,
this hand that directs me,
moving me as a pawn to take down the queen,

I realized that he was always there with me
through all of my past struggles,
acting as a grandmaster
teaching me,
forcing me above the surface,
moving me to be who I was meant to be
in this life all along,

like some central park blitz chess prodigy
or an unearthed mystery,
this daymare visionary,
deep dream, rising killer,
of my toxic mediocrity.

Your Favorite Stranger

Everything starts as a thought
and blossoms from the expectations that are set.
Your mind is a magician,
with the more than occasional, sleight of hand proof.

Your mind is your favorite stranger,
whispering the strangest of certainties to you.
It acts in an illusion,
it acts as a twisting collection of still unproven truths.

Disillusioned at times,
it moves you through the smoke and mirror show,
mirroring back only what you are ready to see,
you must change yourself first,
for your reflection to replicate reality,
the relationship between your thoughts and this world,
is as simple as it could be,

it is, ask and you shall receive,
it is, believe and you will achieve,
it is doubt and shy away
and reality may start to devour you,

your mind is a weighted compass,
all of your most radiant beliefs
and all of your darkest fears
usually end up coming true.

It's what you see

The people at the intersection,
holding signs with the same words for far too long,
I want to paint a portrait of it all,
   and capture the things that are still so wrong,

I've been tangling my perspective,
and twisting it with charm,
but it requires bigger canvases now,
   to sgraffito these visions along,

I try to simplify my image,
chop it into thirds,
blend the colors primarily,
   and capture these fleeting words,

I must create a singular image,
like a manipulated spoon,
reflecting back a Dali elephant legged drawing,
of an electric eel that is shocked
   when it is harpooned.

See,
you can bust our brains repeatedly
and haul us off to sleep,
score our presences tirelessly
   but we won't be scared to dream,

vibrancy is the language that I speak
it wasn't imagined overnight,
magicians never reveal their secrets,
   bluebirds always knows when to fly,

with the endurance of a hunger artist
a tiger may meet me eye to eye,

but I will stare down to the center of his soul
and I will howl, because I feel
      as
      wildly alive.

It always takes the darkness of the night
to see the brilliance that shines in the stars.

the Balance

A light bulb shines from the ceiling
creating a new perspective for me,
the walls are illuminated,
the room in balance,
that computer,
lighting and darkening
over there in the corner of the room,
my words scurry across the floor
off of this bed, and onto the keyboard.

It is this night, stretching so tall, reaching to the stars,
it touches high hopes and the heavens weep,
I hear raindrops tapping at the window,

I move myself to the desk in the living room,
my little escape in the middle of my world,
between my bedroom with my sleeping wife,
and my daughter's room on the other side of the hall,
between everything I know I must be for them,

I find myself with some late-night muse.
I find myself burning a late-night fuse.
I know that it is here that my heart will flood
with these moments of uncertainty.

Yes, some great flood is coming,
it will rid this place of everything that I will not need,
I will continue rocking back and forth here,
swaying with the tides, and I will wait out this storm,
surviving with this twisting melody of thoughts
and waves of consciousness, like the sloshing water outside,

I am sickened by the sea tonight,
the spinning of this expansive sphere,

the twisting motions of day and night,
dividing here and tomorrow,
balancing destiny between my drive and my purpose.

I will wake up on this wood sanctuary,
in this place of solitude,
I will wake up on this desk,
dreaming of the storms that can shake the sea,

and I will write down the visions of my future,
splashing up with all of the ocean's fury,
it will help me to build a world,
out of everything I hold near me now,
most honest and sincere,

I will wake in a bright-lit morning
because the days that are coming
will be the brighter
than any swirling darkness
that can sometimes haunt me,
when the glimpses of my destiny are near.

II – Enchanted Growth

When I close my eyes, I see stars explode,
and wild colors swirling around me.

I am drugs

I
am
drugs,

the
Lisa Frank
electric folded image
of a dolphin
  fluttering spin,

melting
into swirls
of sweet lollipop pinging
  and twisted spiraling sounds,

  flowing
into movements
of colorful wordplay with
sweet aroma phrases.

I drip
sticky
down
  your hands

into
a
broad and open
  parted pathway
  cluttered
  halfway sync,

spinning around
some open-ended

              invitation
to drain myself completely,
of everything that I thought that I knew.

              I
              am
              drugs,

              as
              I
              am
              leaving
              my body,

I see
myself
as some
twisting
folds of space-time,
these tricky tangles of thought
              are so elegantly elaborate,

              I
              see
              myself
              appear and
wash away
into translucent reflection,

into swirls of fluidity,
floating as some dream caught feather,
or notes of a siren melody,
echoing out in an ocean current,
              tempted by the mid summer night's breeze.

Thicker Water

It has started,
the unraveling of life's fabric,
once stitched in the wrinkles
and pockets of time,

I am eroding
in the bathtub,
falling like salt,
to the bottom
of this moment.

But as I begin to settle into this thicker, murky water,
mist rises, and I can feel its tickle on my skin.

I love how I feel right now.

My body rejuvenating, my mind drifting,
a washcloth hangs over my eyes.

Magic surrounds me.

I watch it dissolve
first as seeds of salt,
and it feels smooth as it lines the surface
of who I am.

Always believe in the magic
that flows from your uniqueness.

Soak in it.

For the world will be yours,
when your own magic settles around you.

the Shadowed Work

This well is deep
and its buckets are heavy,
but I am strong,

I look across this landscape
and the fields left to harvest,

I can hear music
and chattered noise
from the people nearby.

I see the twinkling lights,
I feel the immersive buzz as I go to the well,
atop this sacred mound,

I reach down to the center of the earth
and I pull myself back up,

the things that are brought to the surface
will help me to keep believing.

I listen closer now
and hear only chaos in the distance,
from the greener pasture,
and the floodlighting life
of the latest craze.

The town of many sleeps well
while I am awake most of the night,
fighting the shadows that I have made.

If you are hoping for a life of comfort
it is always there for you,
but you are probably making a mistake,

I remain unapologetic
of the shadowed work,
a more fulfilling life will take.

In the fall

A bag of leaves
and fallen feats,
from grown desires
and some fleeting disease,
they are cornered in the alley
but piled high enough,
that ecstasy crumbles
when my toes squeeze.

I'm rolling around
in a bed of dreams,
the colors of lions
in the lying sack of sheets,
I scream in the summer
to Autumn, the daughter of peace,
she awakes in a cold morning,
to a dried out towering scene.

I don't test the wind,
I can't deny my unease
flying in circles,
rushing to the streets,
a bag of old tricks
is spilling clumsily.

I stay humble
as the ghost of Halloween,
even with a poisoned apple,
or a sugar tooth of a treat.

I follow the serenade of a sneeze,
I'm allergic to gesso,
painted skies, and the fall breeze,
life grows underneath the trees,

limbs of consciousness
or succulent seeds,
they are lying upright
for everyone to see.

Meditative timing
that prowess of ease,
some old lessons
are tainting the ground in front of me,
I'm hypnotized, with an out of body experience
still shaking in the nest, a few feet higher than I like to be,

I swing from the branch
my fully extended release,
and pump my legs
as my shoes fly off from my feet,
the fibers of destiny start to unravel,
and my jeans become unstitched at the knees.

Exotic Fruit

It wasn't just a phase
where these thoughts came,
            in sheer bewilderment,

it wasn't just late-night frenzies
that left me feeling overwhelmed, in their haunting nostalgia.

I had wanted to be him
the sorcerer,
enchanting with his spells.

I felt ready to be him
the captain,
bravely championing the sea.

I understand him now
the healer,
miraculous with his touch.

I look to him still
the visionary,
defying old expectation.

Hundreds of hours of work
to chisel out a masterpiece
from a hard chunk of stone,

            with a million rippling thoughts
            boiling closer toward completion
bubbling louder from the unknown,

these aromas of creation
are drawing people closer,
            smelling reminiscent of an old home.

Prepared so exotically
tasting like a dream,
creating lasting impressions
        in their texture and relief.

My words tangle
in your mouth,
please chew but don't choke
        on these seeds,

an existential experience
transforms my sensations,
and moves me closer
        to this unrelenting belief,

that we are seeds of stars first
and able to further the universe's knowledge,
because the magic of creation
        is never out of our own reach.

a Restless Heart

The words
tickle and twitch again,

moving the pen over the paper,
touching my fingers atop the keys
and they dance across the computer screen.

I have impressions
that cut into me
like ink block images,
carving out my periphery.

No matter how you feel
some things are always the same,

the vibrant nature
of creation,

a restless heart,
or the way it can beat
both fast and slow,

or how it fuels creation,
contouring reality,

pressing out repeated images
that never seem to go.

Upon Arrival

Where the honey drips
and the huckleberries roll,
the folds of magnificence
elongating the view,

where the lilies lay down in calm serenity
and life lifts from the waters,
as lush hues of green across these grounds.

Whispers spread
while excitement is in bloom,
the firewood's embers loosen
in the gentle smoky breeze,
blowing toward these big oak-shaded skies.

I look out over the boathouse
floating above the water,
I listen past the growing chirps
and the reaching hums of sound.

I now feel what life can bring
in each new suspension of time,
in the promise of every season
or as each new leaf is turned.

My perspective feels stronger
and more indulgent now,
but I am not overwhelmed
by its scale or its size,

a newfound delicacy
is waking within me,
it blooms in full wonder
and continues to rise.

Passion

A witch blessed and cursed me in this life.
She boiled up a troubling brew
and named it "passion."

Like many of you, I drank it
and it burned my throat
down to the pit of my soul.

I remain compelled by its hell,
this living brew that torments my existence.

For every day, I do not give in
to the passion that grows within me,
my body shakes in revolt,
my mind shutters in doubt,
my emotions toil and turn,
my spirit dances around me,
prodding me to give in to its hell,

either I create during the day,
or I burn in the night.

I burn, burn, burn,
from this spell

passion before peace,
tricked and compelled

uneasy until the end,
it is a blessing of a spell.

the Garden

The veggie seeds
have become a garden,

it has been seven and a half weeks
since they were planted,
and although it's hard to tell every day
they are growing.

It doesn't feel like it
but I have grown too,

sure my hair is wild,
my quads have stretch marks
from the hours of sitting
on my bike trainer
while I am working my job,
pedaling through the day
on my riding desk,
working on the computer.

Sure my hair needs to be cut,
but it doesn't seem important
right now,

no,
not while I am growing,
and I am becoming.

I am learning a lot about myself,
I am taking classes on writing,
I am meditating twice a day,
so my team of spirits, muses and light beings
don't try to speak to me all at once
when I need to rest,

I am reading books on subjects
that I usually would not choose,
on injustice, on empathy, on leadership,

I am challenging myself
and nearly every day I feel uncomfortable,
uncertain, but brand new.

I am not looking behind me much anymore
and I am not too focused on the future,
I am here in growth,
making the meanest glass of lemonade
I ever could make.

I am not rushing anything,
growth takes a lot of work
and I am doing that now,

but the garden is going to outgrow the porch soon,
and I will have to make some choices
on what to cook first.

The wet tomato leaves
smell intoxicating in the sun,
those wild strawberry branches
are crossing over themselves,
the cucumbers aren't here yet,
but their flowers have already bloomed.

The garden is growing
and I am growing too,

but the thing I am most afraid of
is the butterfly actually flying,
when it is finally time
to leave its cocoon.

the Peak

Thousands of hours
to that monumental peak,

mount improbable
mount impossible

mount and dismount,
is how it can feel
sometimes,

I ride this thought
down the twisting reins of the valleys,

I take myself back
into the firefly, spark ready fields,

I mount on this momentum
and ride back up to the sky.

This ascent
may take thousands of hours,

the fight to become
this part of me

under the hats I adorn
and the masks that I display,

a pen rests in my hand
my fingers twitch on these keyboard keys,

and I tremble
at their mercy,

I surrender
to their power,

the spirits muse to me
this certainty,

time ticks
as my body grows older,

thousands of hours
to become the master of my words,

thousands of hours
to become the sorcerer of my spells,

I am dreaming now
of an illuminated prophecy,

where I exist
as this mountain

with wildflower pedals
roaring down the mountainside
in colorful arrays,

the people will climb,
the parties will gather,

mounting up and down my tall faces,
and long lines trek over me,
crossing me,
lining me up and down.

The wind howls up here above the clouds
the cold air is frigid in the winter,

the thunder booms
above my head,

yet, I am strong
and I am still,

you can see my stillness
from thousands of hours away.

I exist
as this still,
stoic,
majestic
accumulation
of earth gathering
over time,

in the night,
I will exist as a beautiful shadow
stretching across the skyline

ready for the sun to rise
and shine so bright
that each time it does
no other stars seem to exist
in that same sky,
at all.

Destiny shines

Destiny shines
as a sunrise,

its bright rays reach
into the pockets of the ocean,

it makes the sands reflect as gold
from broken down peaks,

and the purple sky bows
in destiny's majestic presence,
before it lifts in a final retreat,

colors change
when destiny rises
in the skyline,

it brightens the world so much
that even the smallest buds
of forgotten seeds,

can be called a miracle,
when they grow up wildly enough
to finally be seen.